W9-BSY-823

Saint Peter's University Library
Withdrawn

In Time and Place

Johns Hopkins: Poetry and Fiction
John T. Irwin, General Editor

In Time and Place

John Hollander

The Johns Hopkins University Press
Baltimore and London

This book has been brought to publication with the generous assistance of the G. Harry Pouder Fund and the Albert Dowling Trust.

© 1986 The Johns Hopkins University Press
All rights reserved
Printed in the United States of America

The Johns Hopkins University Press, 701 West 40th Street,
Baltimore, Maryland 21211
The Johns Hopkins Press Ltd., London

∞ The paper used in this publication meets the minimum requirements of American National Standard for Information Sciences — Permanence of Paper for Printed Library Materials, ANSI Z39.48–1984.

Library of Congress Cataloging-in-Publication Data

Hollander, John.
  In time and place.

  (Johns Hopkins, poetry and fiction)
  I. Title.
PS3515.03485I55   1986   813'.54   86-45438
ISBN 0-8018-3392-2 (alk. paper)
ISBN 0-8018-3393-0 (pbk.: alk. paper)

Some of the verse and prose in this book has been published previously, in different form and with different titles, as follows:

"A Glimpse of Proserpina" appeared in *The New Yorker,* "Looking East in Winter" and "Vintage Absence" in *Poetry.* Other sections of *In Time* appeared in *The New Republic, New York Review of Books, Partisan Review, America, Southwest Review, Michigan Quaterly Review, 2 + 2, Kentucky Poetry Review,* and *Verve.*

Part of *In Between* first appeared in *Parenthese,* then all of it in *Raritan,* under the title "From an Old Notebook". All of *In Place* was first printed in a limited edition by Harry Duncan at Abattoir Editions, Omaha. "Building a Tower" and "Crossing Water" were included in *Spectral Emanations* (Atheneum Publishers, 1979); permission to reprint is acknowledged.

PS
3515
.03485
I55
1986

for Richard Howard

Contents

Desire, the Other, Loss, the World of Now and Then, give way in time to Here and There, the *where*'s which mime the *who*'s among which we are hurled by virtue merely of being in and among ourselves: then place will represent the absent face, lost voices hum in scenes, in seeing itself; as firm lines decompose into grim dust that never sings, their Truth shakes ashes from its wings and rises once more into prose.

In Time

Valentine's Day Has Come and Gone

There was an end to hearts and rhymes,
The old occasion rushed on past.
Now? Unruled pages, and the vast
Spaces of our unsinging times

Within which these still measured lines
Shall wander yet, slowly to mark
A journey through a kind of dark
In which a distance faintly shines.

Half-Empty Bed Blues I

Lying here underneath a sheet,
Clothed with my wet, unsleeping skin,
I hear my breathing deep within
The rustling ghost of you I greet.

This wide bed is my body: take
It and lie in it, that your heart
May beat against its sheets, and start,
Like my poor trembling limbs, to shake.

These pale tears are my mumbled-over
Wine: take them and drink, and when
I'm dry of sorrow once again,
Eye my drained glasses, and discover

How, empty, they will only mirror
The vacancy of shape you leave
Each evening, when your spectres weave
Another coverlet of terror.

An Inchstone

A long strong week is up, of bright
Mornings and quiet, joyless eves:
This neither celebrates nor grieves,
But marks a solemn *Wocheszeit*;

A candle in an ugly glass
To light the day your presence died
And various ghosts were born, who hide
And wait for other weeks to pass,

Then, though unsummoned, will emerge
By day, at night and in between.
What was here, and what should have been
Breathe hoarsely in a soundless dirge.

Now a new cycle must unfold,
Again, familiar daylight bare
The calendar's impartial stare,
The clock's hands, neither warm nor cold.

Looking East in Winter

I walk on Sixty-ninth Street toward
The leafless trees and distant towers
Across the bare park, ruined bowers
Revealing more than summer's hoard

Of dusty, rich, green leaves would show:
Not merely the bare fact of tree
But, glimpsed across a vacancy
Of air and rocky field below,

A vision of eventual heights
Touched by the sunlight's sinking hand,
Not given us in a fine land
Or a time choked with green delights.

Yet what is gold but hope of green?
And rhyming cold but hope deferred?
A scruffy and unsinging bird
Alights in some dark in-between.

The Ruminants

The pastures of remembering
Are over-grazed by now; the slow
Mute beasts of sorrow come and go
(Bare patches wait for some new spring),

Solemnly ruining the text
Of sad anteriors and joys
In valleys blanketed from noise:
What page of our tale will go next?

In my high, dreaming car, I steer
Away, and here I wake to light:
Lashed with cold rains, the hills of night,
The shores of morning, washed with fear.

Half-Empty Bed Blues II

The cold, gray morning floods the sleep
Where you have been with me: I hear,
Outside, the dead march of the year;
Within, I am too chilled to weep.

Even in the undreaming dark
The spectre of your absence, true
To my bed, plumper some than you,
Quite vanishes and leaves no mark,

But then creeps back in the thick dawn
To fill the circle of my arms
With nothing, and the loud alarms
Of heartbeat wake me and are gone.

And so she will return, until
The kindness of perpetual night
Puts all our absences to flight
Forever, as it ever will,

That final comforter, a shroud
Wherein a night of sleep's a stitch:
This is the coldest sense in which
Death joins the patient with the proud.

Half-Empty Bed Blues III

The stalks of heavy waiting droop:
Old Cronos' scythe, a chronic error,
Is not the mirror of my terror;
I see Time with a rounded scoop

Who, while I sleep the sleep of earth
Hollows me out, of hope and rest;
Awake, I grope for absent breast,
And belly fled, those mounds of dearth.

And lie flat on this plain of lack,
Desire contriving no escapes.
A yawn, but not of boredom, gapes
Below my sad, bewildered back.

When Song Will Not Do

Across the street a tenor whine
— The voice too thick, piano thin —
Praises *die schöne Müllerin*
Who, as he shrieks, *ist sein, ist sein*;

I slam the window down, to hear
Your absence in the settling dust,
Wondering at the Miller's lust:
Wandering echoes in my ear . . .

In the dim song of distances
The river silently unwinds,
Your soft mill tirelessly grinds
The mixture of your joys and his;

I hear the laughing overshot
Wheel and its merry, whispered splashing,
The moan of softening, the mashing
Pestle gentle in your pot.

Cold as a millstone, the wide bed,
Unheeded, all my unground grain
Heaped up in waste, or spilled in pain
In full sight of the still unfed.

Slowly I play through *Loath to Depart**
By Farnaby; the now-in-tune
Piano saves, from my rough-hewn
Graces and runs, the fragile art

Of varying a common theme
While keeping on familiar ground
(Mine based on loss). I have not found
What variation might redeem;

So these divisions weep out woe,
A false relation here and there,
A sharp pain after natural care
From whose plain text these fancies grow.

*♩♩♩|○♩|♩·♩♩|○·|

Footnote to One of These Notes

Why rhyme? And why for this most late
And serious of texts: have I
Not saved such verse to jollify,
Upbraid, goad, and commemorate?

— The tone of what the left hand writes:
Not the more deeply cadenced mode
That must abjure the rhymer's code
And the sharp closures it invites.

Why rhyme? To make it harder? But
Harder to what? Harder to tell
The truth when timed by such a bell,
When files of words are labeled "Shut"?

To make it easier to hum
Comforting songs against the blast
Of cold, wind, loss and undone past,
And hollow wailings yet to come?

The wandering pathways of the verse
Secret occasions lose me in
End as unmarked as they begin;
In such rich woods all trails disperse.

No: "poetry nothing affirms"
As Sidney said, "and cannot lie";
We live *vers libre,* but come to die
In something like rhyme's final terms.

And thus, as death serves as a hedge
Around life, my imprisoned words
(Yoked to the task, not caged like birds)
Keep to the center, keep their edge.

Telling Fortune

Chicken tonight. I reach inside
A half-prepared bird and remove
The packaged entrails: will they prove
To be a haruspicious guide?

For want of you and readings of
The body's texts, I turn to signs:
Planets, conjunctions, stars and trines,
Perplexing all my house of love . . .

I wonder what my palm will say;
Walking across the frozen park,
I still consult the book of dark
Bare branches etched against the gray.

But now, this giblet magic quelled
By the quotidian's quack-quack,
I turn from divination, back
To evidence of signs withheld.

An Introduction to Absence

"Absence," Fulke Greville says, "is pain".
I flee it through the gates of sleep;
Discount therefore the tears I weep
A propos of the falling rain.

My sobbing, at the sunset hour,
Half-rhymes with distant pistol shots
Re-echoing from chimney-pots
And the round, nearby water tower.

Lacrimae rerum, and their thin
Counterparts in my sorrow, cry
Not for my loss: that leaves a dry
And silent emptiness within,

A hall deserted even by
Pain, which is presence, after all,
Of dark intruding waves which crawl
In at the hand or at the eye.

Absence is presence, then, we learn,
Joined by the middle term of pain.
You gone, only such jokes remain.
Et excrucior. And I burn.

The One and the Many

Your right hand, raised to make me halt,
Gave me untendered solitude
(Now ravens bring me sorrow's food,
The bread of life without the salt).

I am no sooner used to new
Modes of an old aloneness when
Your left hand takes it back again
And leaves me among swarms of you:

Thus on the avenues in crowds
Ghosts of you in the distance stride
Toward me, and shivering spectres hide
In bed among the bones and shrouds

Of sheets and limbs. Put them to flight
From that wide, cold, half-emptied field!
Touch me, exile them all, and yield
Me up you, and my *Einsamkeit.*

A Talk in the Park

"With thee conversing I forget
All time," Eve said to Adam; so
Would I to you: but time shall mow
The living grass where we are met

In the sparse park amid the hiss
Of crawling traffic, where your talk
Leads me for a brief space to walk
In bowers of artificial bliss.

Unchanging winds blow through the leaves
(Lips that may whisper but not kiss);
Yet time remembers us in this:
Our words are reaped and bound in sheaves,

And gathered in and stored in dense
Dark granaries for winter feasts:
Slow, kind, uncomprehending beasts
Will eat our words in innocence.

Alone I'll watch through hardened, iced
Winter sun, in that hay-day of
The fallen green of hope and love,
Shivering and unparadised.

The Looking-glass of Grief

The blind use slim and silent canes
That tap-tap-tap no more to mark
The noisy surface of the dark
On avenues, in subway trains.

I stare into their eyes to see
Myself completely mirrored there:
Silvered eyes should return my stare
Better than clear ones reading me.

Even a stagnant pool reflects
A dim daguerreotype, but blind
Eyes mirror nothing of the kind
That the inquiring eye expects.

So the clear, morning landscape, dulled
By absence more than visionary
Turns a blind eye in which the very
Light of my own gaze was annulled.

A String of Rubies

The semi-precious gems I've sent,
Emaux et camées, opals, red
Garnets laid in a fretwork bed
Of pinchbeck rhymes, well-made, well-meant,

Lie dully in their box, appalled
By how they must be reappraised
At time of pain or, chilled and dazed
By the green fire of emerald

So bravely worn in their despite
Whose color opens up the road —
I should have given gems that showed
A stopping and a startling light.

While my love fretted, aged and slept,
Thou by the Indian Ganges side
Didst emeralds find; I by the tide
Of Hudson in the sunset wept.

These tears that redden as they fall
In the departing western light
Might have become mere jets of night,
Dark mirrors but without recall.

Time's slow lithogeny alone
Could not have made their forms complete
But under pressure and great heat
The drops have hardened into stone,

And glistering tears no longer run
Down faces, but make sorrow known
In many faces of their own.
Here are your rubies, one by one:

A moment of red sunset dying
Remembered as a point of red,
Pierced through by changing lights that said
SPRY was for baking, and for frying.

◇

A ruby drop of dreaming rain —
Caught by the stop-light of the car
Ahead, with Louisville too far
To drive — wakens and dries in pain.

◇

The pale gouts of spilled Beaujolais
Too innocent to have acquired
Much taste, but all that we desired
Then, or for which we then could pay.

◇

The listening, wise spot of light
Set in the amplifier's frame
Though hardly an eternal flame
Glowed yet throughout the early night.

◇

A battered bead of reddened glass
Dropped from some funeral ornament
Rolling on the bare stage: it meant
That a bright night had come to pass.

◇

Clustered reflectors on the cars
Parked at a party where you danced
And wept and wandered, chose and chanced
By the fire, out below the stars

(How shall we read those pigeon's-blood
Stones in a drop: a bleeding dove
Of wounded Peace? or failing Love?
Burnt Olive? Myrtle in the mud?)

◇

An ember bluer far than flame,
Emblem of love uncooled yet late
That lingered on below the grate
On Wonder Street when morning came,

Unread for its erotic truth:
For, dying coals with greater heat
Than fire? — children of Wonder Street
Could not imagine more than youth.

◇

A chain of drops of ruby port
Postprandial, on Monday nights,
Aperitif to the delights
Of bringing home to you the sort

Of talk on which we fed our souls
And slaked our thirsty minds for years,
As the breath of our eyes and ears
Fanned blackened and dead, whitened coals

To mental color, in the seats
Of *U.T., Brattle, Symphony*
(All this old footage for you — see
It redden at my wild conceits!)

◇

What gem is there I cannot give?
Ruddy Aldebaran proclaims
(As once above the minor Thames,
Staring at darkness through a sieve

Of summer stars we saw it do)
The high pursuit of radiance (he's
One who pursues the Pleiades).
Now he's one ruby more for you.

Precious jewel of my Scorpion,
Antares glittered in July
Then in the clear New Hampshire sky
A star nearby, a falling one,

Acknowledged tears that you had dropped
In darkness there, and those which I
Would weep under a winter sky
Years later when your love had stopped.

A red lamp than outran the dark
While swinging in among the stars,
Perched on our steamer's metal spars,
Not rising like a hopeless spark.

A distant flash of winking, bright
Gem from across the starlit bay's
Cold, corresponding dark repays
Ancient attention now with light.

A planetary spot of red:
High at the top of Bergamo,
Hopeful, it rose above the snow
(A child was being put to bed.)

SAINT PETER'S COLLEGE LIBRARY
JERSEY CITY. NEW JERSEY 07306

A trucker's taillight rushing past
Our gray car spinning on the ice
(Nature, gathering up her dice,
Looked elsewhere for another cast).

Here ends my worded strand of gems,
As diamonds darken with the day
And all *les bijoux indiscrets*
Forsake their chattering diadems.

Its name encoding a command,
Each ruby in your memory, very
Tiny, and anagrammed to "bury"
May store up warmth in a cold land,

While my yet-vivid flames remain
Burning inside that furnace where
These gems were synthesized of air
Of love of memory and pain:

The deepest treasures mined, you see,
Shall not even before I've done
(Passionate lapidary pun)
Rue the bare year that comes to *be*.

A Defense of Rhyme

Because there is too much to say
I cast it into such a form
As this, to keep your hearing warm
On my love's silent, chilly day.

Not that you need the hollow chime
Of these old bells to make you hear,
But lest each thought run on a year
Or more, some measure must keep time.

This succedancum and prop
May signal truth's infirmities,
But chanting chokes on its own lees
And rhymed lines know best when to stop.

Orpheus Alone

I sought you out deep in the cave
Of desolation for a while;
You followed me for half a mile
Out into sunlight, past the grave.

Where did I pause in joy? and when
Was the bad moment I looked back
To see you framed against the black
Welcoming gates of hell again?

Now if attendant rocks have heard
My sad arpeggios they've ignored them;
Tree-petals fall because I bored them;
My songs touch neither beast nor bird,

Nor reach down past attendant shades
Into that lower darkness bright
For you with its dim, altered light,
To where, in one of those black glades

I know by hearsay, you remain
Imprisoned by the Winter Queen
Herself half-captive. Here in green
Glades that now flourish in disdain

Of my deploring song I wait
For my cracked lyre to crawl away
In silent tortoise-hood some day,
For love to waddle off like hate.

Vintage Absence

Down on the closet's darkened floor
Slumbering in their litres lie
Wines we could once afford to buy:
Is it you they are waiting for?

The '61 Brane-Cantenac
Keeps getting better as it grows
Treasures within its taste, which those
Fine '66s long will lack.

But I'll drink up the thin new wine
Of Beaujolais, grown pink with tears:
Its life-span briefer than a year's,
Its flavor something less than fine.

But what lie somewhere in between . . .
Each week I meditate upon
Dark bottles that have come and gone
To teach what readiness can mean.

Patience and Longing (for the taste
That will not yield to longing and
Loves the cool undemanding hand
Of patience) lay my cellar waste,

With green, disastrous drinks and brown,
Leathery ghosts laid down too long.
My heart is ever ripe, but wrong:
Long has no vintage of renown.

My deeper spirits then must keep
(The lighter fancies have been drained)
And some day what will have remained,
By moonlight sipped, will guard our sleep.

After a Sad Talk

The young leaves shiver in their green
Chill, as the broad gray sky exhales
Rough winds, although the time entails
A mellow heat that might have been.

An early visitation from
Recumbent summer, leaping spring
Having sped by, flapped a hot wing
And fled this cold park where we come

To a cold parting once again,
Meeting unjoined, two not together.
Suppose, though, that the late May weather
Flamed with approaching June, what then?

Or that a sudden fall of thunder
Had driven us indoors, that neat
Cold revelations on the street
Might have been hidden yet in wonder?

Oh, the sure cold would claim its own
In time, whatever dreams of green
Warmed by our paired repose might mean.
The ground between us turns to stone.

Down the Chute

Time to drop off the mail again,
Without a moment to emend
The text I had composed to send;
And yet the moment needs my pen

To represent it now. My fears
And anger and desire and lonely
Hopelessness today could only
Blank my ball-point; yet all those tears

Once served as ink for older quills.
I must keep up my love for you
In a commercial, skyey blue
Which neither drops, nor dries, nor spills,

But, hardened like accustomed sorrow,
Tirelessly erodes away,
Sketching out all my woes today,
Yielding its picture up tomorrow.

After Blossoming

The text of early spring snipped up
By idle scissors lies like white
Papery apple petals quite
Unblossomed from their common cup,

As if still moralizing, glum
About What May Not Be Enjoyed,
Some dada cutup had destroyed
A homely florilegium,

Fallen and scattered on the path
Yet wholly plain to ears that hear
Foot (hushed in petal) fall, to clear
Eyes that see through to aftermath.

Envisioned flowers in their turn
Became prophetic leaves, and sank
Their fragments of a general blank
Down to the bed where eyes that burn

With searching grief will always find
Their abjects. All my sybilline
Readings of which could ever mean
Is in their *foliae rasae,* blind

And thus, if not all-seeing, then
Any-seeing at least. All last
Weekend the lusty chestnut cast
Flowery towers groundward. When

They still went trembling in the breeze
I yet compared me to a spring
Day, warmed or chilled by varying
Winds which both buffeted the trees

And led them out of sullen bud
Into the brave, white blossoms — those
I sought to read while my heart froze,
And still peruse there in the mud.

Spring is done, and I may have wept
Too much, but have outlasted it,
Construing in the ruined writ
Of petals dropped, a promise kept.

Special Sessions

Imprisoned in this court of law,
I hear the guarded lawyers drone
On in a halting monotone
And may not even read or draw,

But, the sole juror of my case,
Sequestered in my present fate,
Wearily I deliberate
The future's bleak and silent face.

Though turnkey Time may set me free
From dark courts of the loins and heart,
I shall not ever have "the part
Of Justice, which is Equity".

Waiting is virtue, act is crime
In life where justice is reversed:
For me the sentence has come first,
The verdict will emerge in time.

The Fetch

The insubstantial corpse that stayed
Behind you when you finally fled
Has walked these rooms and filled my bed
With empty dreams, a ghost unlaid:

Even now, as whole cups of tears
Have dried into the usual air
And I may meet you here and there,
That spirit, moist with life, appears

Where someone else may bathe my wound
In the bright fountain of her smile,
Warming the darkness for a while
In a room shadowed but unmooned.

I see you even in the most
Guarded of places, in her bed
Fucking there with another ghost
Under the bedclothes of my head.

What character must I erase —
Initial N, leaving A ME
For a name? — to send on its way
This golem with your hands and face?

The Old Scribe

No muses have deserted me:
Spring waters murmur in me yet.
What is the loss I must forget?
— My memory, Mnemosyne,

Who kept the outlines clear, distinct
Of what had been and what was said
While my book of the gone and dead
Was crudely penned and vaguely inked.

Yours was to have been there for all
These years, the binding bent a bit,
The pages foxed, its holy writ
Intact through all that can befall

What is preserved in text. To read
Each page over is still to hear
A voice replenishing my ear
With what it will forever need:

The record, ever sweetly sung,
As once, now, of the radiant past,
Calling my way across the vast
Futures I wander, blind, among.

In Fine Print

The clean, white sheets and the black cat
Await my narrowed body now;
The room, the presence they allow
— Falsely generous, for all that —

Compose a chamber of precise
Dreaming and certain vision. Here
I have revisited this year:
Bêtes-noires among my Edelweiss,

Departures, losses, even new
Emptyings of a partially
Refilled cup — as I seemed to see
A tall veiled girl (no ghost of you)

Leaving me for a former friend.
Uncolored dreams like these declare
What their beholders cannot bear
To keep invisible; they end

In waking to a world of water
Color, the black-and-white of dream
Softened by a more fluent gleam
Brushed in by Sleep's fair younger daughter.

From a House Party

Here in this splendid, silly room —
Mullions and oaken linenfold —
The past aped by the rather old —
My ear in pain, my heart in gloom,

Beneath the faint sneer of Augustus
(Above me stands his marble head)
I read that Audrey G. is dead,
Likewise, the bearded J. R. Justice.

I sorrow in this pine-green air.
Back where you are, garbage and thugs
Abound, the cats tear up the rugs,
The summer's shadows grow. Somewhere

A dropped glass smashes on the floor;
The household-gods are breaking up.
Soon there will be one last cracked cup
And I shall love you all the more

As now, so much more than I could
Then, when we bound ourselves to — what?
— Unbrokenness we thought our lot,
Children of the enchanted wood.

Forms of Address

We keep learning of violences.
Your salutation reads: "Dear J
H" (and the pain in-jammed), to say
Something of what half-silence is.

What ails our correspondence now
Comes down to first forms of address,
Avoiding any old caress
Or touch of term that would allow

Only of feelings sealed in those
Epistles of our former state.
We telephone across the great
Divide; we've used the silent rose;

I scribble these in rhyming prose;
I reach through darkness: no dial tone
Comes from the telekardion
Whose circuits now may never close.

"Dear J H" — one of the few "Dear — "'s
(I realize now: we never were
Apart, save for the dreadful stir
Long in your heart) I've had in years.

To have arrived at writing letters
So late and unaccustomedly
Sadly suggests that only we
Are now our elders and our betters.

"Dear [initials]"? "Oh, [Name]"? "Dear Friend"?
(All true. One, adequate. Two, thin.)
You don't know quite how to begin?
I meditate on ways to end.

I Was Wrong, You See . . .

Always Time's arguments refute us:
What classic ignorance had led
Me to think an Augustan head
Turns out to be a bust of Brutus;

And what I thought my love had sealed
Is broken open, and the curse
Written, in secret ink, in verse,
Darkening slowly, is revealed;

And Time has made me comprehend
The two poor ghosts we've come to be:
Loss, swallowing its mystery,
Desire, feeding on its end.

Others Who Have Lived in This Room

Why have I locked myself inside
This narrow cell of four-by-four,
Pacing the shined, reflecting floor
Instead of running free and wide?

Having lost you, I'd rather not
Be forced to find my way as well
In the broad darkness visible
Of prose's desert, vast and hot;

But in the shade of these four walls
Bounce the black ball of my despair
Off each in turn, and spurn the glare
Outside the cool, confining halls.

Why, then, if so ascetic, a
Rich game? Why must I always play
The stanza called *abba*
In books of *ars poetica*?

Avoiding hollow chime or cant,
The false narration and invalid
Wails of the modern form of ballad,
Less of a song and more a chant,

Accented crotchets, semi-brave
Measures of resonance will suit
Laying the painfully acute
Finalities beside the grave.

The daughters' measures may surprise,
The Mother Memory can amuse,
But *Abba*'s spirit must infuse
The form which will memorialize.

"Memorialize" . . . But who is dead?
The unstressed "and" of "wife and man"?
Its life was measured by the span
As by the act, a word unsaid

That sleeps with memory and John
Hollander's long unpublished poem,
And will yet rise from its mute home
In textual sepulchre anon.

This rhyme of mirrored halves arose
Headless from the ashes of
Phoenix and his constant dove
Intestate else, as Shakespeare shows:

"So they loved as love in twain
Had the essence but in one;
Two distincts, division none:
Number thus in love was slain."

Sidney and Sandys when they gave alms
To Sion's muse, and called upon
Strophes that purled through Helicon,
Used it to paraphrase the Psalms;

Herbert of Cherbury employed
The same form to determine whether
Love could continue on forever
After mere bodies were destroyed,

Writing, *"in her up-lifted face*
Her eyes which did that beauty crown
Were like two starrs that having faln down,
Look up again to find their place."

Our stanza with a great to-do
Warned the seducer to be wary
And thus (trochaically) by Carew
(Or, as the learned say, Carew):

"Stop the chafèd Bore, or play
With the Lyons paw, yet feare
From the Lovers side to teare
Th'Idoll of his soul away."

Then Marvell's Daphnis, turning down
His never-yielding Chloe's last
Frantic attempt to hold him fast
By finally rucking up her gown:

"Whilst this grief does thee disarm,
All th'Enjoyment of our Love
But the ravishment would prove
Of a Body dead while warm."

Filling these decorous and deep
Cups of rhyme, Jonson's "Elegy"
Lay still; draining their melody,
Rossetti dreamed his sister's sleep.

Shores the Virgilian river laves
Crossed with the sounding of the bar
Out in the North Sea, heard afar
Graven in Keatsian beating waves;

Heard by the voice that filled these rooms
With sounds of mourning, cries of hope
Escaped love's fire, in a trope
Of marriage, memory and tombs

Of faith deceased, to which he fled
From touch not taken, half-recalled
Stillborn caresses that appalled
The poet, not the loving dead.

I, too, fill up this suite of rooms,
A bit worn now, with crowds of word,
Hoping that prosody's absurd
Law can reform the thoughts it dooms;

An emblem of love's best and worst:
Marriage (where hand to warm hand clings,
Inner lines, linked by rhyming rings);
Distance between the last and first),

This quatrain is born free, but then
Handcuffed to a new inner sound,
After what bliss it may have found
Returns to the first rhyme again.

— Not our bilateral symmetry,
But low reflecting high, as on
His fragile double poised, the swan:
What's past mirrored in what will be.

O, Once I Had Thyme of My Own

These cracked hands, gloved in history,
Were like a bumbling gardener's, who
Kept the herbaceous borders true
But bruised the flowers terribly.

Pressures that made the petals shrink,
Remembered in the nervous root,
Bore as it were a barren fruit
Breeding a new Lamarckian pink

— This flower with a sense of fear
Of husbandry grown deep within;
And you, poor Flora, raking in
Those ruined patches, shrunk and sere.

Despair for all the floral parts.
But do not let the gardener go:
Before, behind, between, below,
His tender hands may quicken yet

The delicatest buds of doubt,
The lovely stigma petaled round,
The warmest regions underground —
The garden will itself cry out!

Those hands will sow in love anew
That reaped in damaged joy before,
And sink, soft to the grassy floor,
As if from the fresh balm of dew.

They Failed. (But To Do What?)

Even cheap marble, and the gilt
Monuments in museums will
Outlast these verses and the skill
And sorrow with which they were built,

Not graven to eternize you
In the bright adamant of myth,
Nor high, protesting monolith
Ever to wail and plead and sue;

Nor yet scrawled in the wave-damp sand
While a chill wind warns as it numbs,
Till the erasing breaker comes
And claims you with its bits of land;

But written in the speaking tongue,
The neck, the breast, the legs apart
— Those scattered regions of the heart,
The gardens which truth grows among.

Guard these few leaves of the late mail
That they may live as long as you,
Their whisperings forever new,
Blown abroad only if they fail.

The Constant Fisherman

These lines I cast into the blue
Sea have entrapped no treasure yet:
No smudge-faced marble Venus, wet
With tears of spray: no trace of you,

No answering tug along the line —
As if each end-word's final touch
Had found a rhyme in you to clutch —
Run, trembling, through the wind and brine.

But still I cast, till darkness lends
My line a curve: the moon above
Slackens the water and my love.
My line is silent at both ends;

Weary of the uncaught, it ends
Its search, and doubling slowly back
Bends into nets of love and lack
That sleepy patience guards and mends.

Steady Work

You have no book of me beside
Your new bed now, and what you read
Is not of shadow but of deed
And having done, not having died.

But argument can dull the soul
And even wisdom's rod may tire
While, hammered out in fancy fire
My sharp lines, whispering, unroll.

And so, like paper airplanes sent
Across the room in grammar school,
I shoot these off against the rule
Toward your new disestablishment.

But even though a well-drawn pen
Make each line hit the mark it seeks,
It will take more than a few weeks
To rhyme you back to bed again.

Shutting Up Shop

Now, silence for a while, the still
Work of days, loneliness of nights;
Spilled trivia would choke delights
If there were any left to kill.

With fluttering heart and no success
Poor Psyche sorted seeds, but sick
Of Love's mad tasks, I turn to pick
My way through piles of dailiness.

In Between

I must learn to live here more. Sleep, illness, death are all horizontal, and while we are alive the ground, the surface of beds, the tabletops, the horizon itself — heaven knows, these are more than enough of a reminder. (But suppose that we all slept, and died, standing upright in deep, narrow grooves: should we then value standing the less, have no mixed repugnance and longing to fall down to the position of lying?) But these horizontals, these patient, pale blue lines, are like amenable benches in a bare and featureless park, on which to rest is a liveliness.

*

How to misuse a notebook:

> *Put a secret in it*
> *Tell yourself a lie in it*
> *Plan an act of violence in it*
> *Wipe a pen in it*
> *Carry it visibly about*
> *Dance on its lines as if before a mirror*
> *Keep telephone numbers, for assignations, in it*

All of these misuses are of the order of chewing its leaves for a mad salad; they are like eating fruit that has been hung on the tree with one, not for one — fruit to be understood for its deep light, rather than its mere sweetness (which indeed, inhered in everything else). This would be the fruit of the tree that was one's own inversion, its head sucking the ground, its arms reaching for depth. This would be the figurative fruit, the result and the consequence, which it was eating one's own future to consume. So that after all it is not a matter of living here more. It is more a matter → in this bright place of the page, unshadowed save for the cool bower cast by my own hand — of learning to dwell.

*

I must try to return daily to this house. Why have I kept it up for so long, paying the taxes of disaster, the ruinous heating bills (all those unused rooms whose radiators warm nothing but spaces, and yet cannot be shut off), only to pay it uneasy and impulsive visits? I could let out rooms, but nobody seems to want them — they are, after all, peculiarly cramped, and who understands that rooms which have insufficient room in them thereby bestow much more than even openness could provide?

*

Back here after quite a few days away. There has been a blizzard: I have been confined to the house, which has itself become a house of snow — gables reshaped into softly curved forms, streets silent of passage. But it is only today that I could make the inland trek back here. Opening pages unlocks them; the only locks here are those of the will-not-to-open, but those are very strong. The pages have been locked away from the room in which they lie, as the room is locked away from the snow outside it. Yet suppose that both enclosures were ruptured, that snow blew through the window onto the open pages. What then? Why, nothing: this ink will not run, and the damp can be blotted away, and nothing would have blown into the pages as it did into the room. Or, Why, everything: the surface of the page is the scene of writing. Suppose, too, that we consider again the philosopher writing of speech-acts. He sneezes loudly: what then? Why, nothing. Why, everything — unless he claims the sneeze as an example and writes of it directly. In that case, the whole anecdote would be as pointless as my own, now, which asks of the weather's sneeze of snow through the room ('tain't a fit night out for man nor beast) *in what way it comes as a trace of something beyond, and not merely external.*

*

Today the sky in gradations imperceptible from deep, grave blue falling into pallor, dipping further into sand, finally sunk into rose. As if the spectrum had been taken back, and this bow of broken promise handed us in return. In the late, gray light my almost-emptied cup falls over; on the bare desk beside my page lies a pool of the pine-dark tea. To touch the pool of consciousness directly, like Hegel, is so to disturb its surface that it can no longer reflect. We who keep our fingers dry can only employ those touching tropes of contact — looking, considering, picturing, describing, invoking — so that in the continually unruffled surface the figures of depth will remain strong.

*

I visit less and less. I wonder which of us — the Old Place? Me? — is forsaking the other. It's never that easy to figure out. In any case, I came back today merely to give the pages an airing; they regard me blankly and uninvitingly like sheets of a sickbed. This must be all for today. The next time I return, and thenceforth, I shall write only in invisible ink.

It works! The secret ink is a success! After having tried several compounds of lemon juice and what-have-you, I concocted a clear fluid from dried tears, some sweat from this morning's fit of anxiety as I peered through the half-open study door and saw the mess of unanswered mail, a bit of fine white wine that had gone beyond all hope and faith, and drops of remembered rain that had fallen once between two touching faces. As I wrote the second word of this entry, "works," the first one had already begun to disappear into the silence of unfilled page. What I can write here now has immediate consequences only. In purity and true power it surpasses anything I have ever put down on paper, for

1. It is unreadable, save for a brief moment, and then by one authentic reader only — myself, as I will be in the next few seconds. Not my ungrateful offspring, my self that reads this a month later in a state of self-satisfied distance and distaste. Not some glossy editor, annotating my remarks with a surfeit of *cf.*'s. Not those multitudes who will survive me, unwitting of how even greater will be the multitudes who are to drown *their* memories.

2. It can bring forth only the next word, not the next thing or the next deed. It can bring about only its own syntactical fulfillment.

3. It can never be caught out in a lie. Neither can it be grossly verified.

4. It is a way of writing filled with the presence of the present. It keeps up with the times, as journalism must, even as Time keeps up with it — firmly but justly cleaning up after it with his great industrial vacuum, so that not even a scrap of fibbing involving "outlive," "outlast," or "much later on" is left to do its dirty business.

So — I can return to this place now without the usual ballet variation of backtracking into which journals are led (viz., "Little did I know when I wrote those last lines what would happen the next evening, after dinner, when Lord B. turned to me with his astonishing suggestion"; or "So much for good intentions! This morning at breakfast I could not keep myself from — " or "Cancel that. I must somehow not have meant it; by lunch time today I realized that — "). I can walk into the rooms I had shut off to save heat and not just look around for a moment, retrieve an odd volume of Emerson lying on a chair, and leave for a more comfortable place. I can visit here now without prejudice and with no need for reproach. I am pleased; but perhaps I should be less casual and more deeply grateful. Imagine having discovered how to live without making constant messes as we all do, with every delicious moment leaving a nasty dried cake on some utensil, every fruitful impulse resulting in piles of crumpled paper and surfaces covered with books, cards, coffee cups, boxes, clippings, dust, and old spectacles. Imagine that — no residues, no excretions, no untidy aftermath, nothing unpaid or forgotten. One should be insanely grateful for that. And yet all I can feel for having been allowed my discovery is a certain delighted satisfaction, a feeling that of course I deserved something like this, and that it better damned well have happened when it did, before too much longer.

So — here I can visit again, dwell again. There will be nothing left to embarrass or rebuke me, nothing for me to condemn. Only (faintly yellowed — this is an old book) white space, blue lines, a faint red vertical on each numbered page, growing day by day, more and more widely separating the place where I am now from the last entry, my last visible words: *The next time I return, and thenceforth, I shall write only in invisible ink.*

*

Last night it struck me — as I awoke from sleep to hear one of the cats (the black? the gray?) padding down the uncarpeted stairs — that the day might come when morning

would relinquish its hold on sanity and light. I could
almost feel it shrugging wearily, dropping an opened hand,
crying out "*Ach!* there has been too much." The night that
had surrounded such a day: would it accept the gift of
light? the burden of clear consciousness? the problem of
health? Where else could they go? Whither would they fall,
or rise?

*

A trace, a single mark, has defaced the trail of silence I
have been leaving behind me. Dust? A flyspeck? In any
case, adhering to the first, now invisible, stroke, the first
letter I wrote several days ago. A vertical stroke. The trace
of visible darkness along it — a long spot, as it were — is like
a moment of hoarse breath in a thicket of stillness.

*

This place — this house to which I now seem dutifully to be
returning — has become a watchtower. From it I look out
into things. Being figurative, its walls are neither here nor
there; its windows are the eyes of the space within it. Like
all watchtowers, this is also a beacon, sweeping the
horizon, or the nearby trees, with the beam of awareness.

And yet it is not easy precisely to define the condition of
seeing the world from a place like this. Indoors and out-
doors have been continuously and uneasily wedded since
the former was conceived by our first parents as they hid
themselves amid the trees of their garden. Outdoors has no
meaning until it has first been read through windows from
within: only then will its spaciousness descend upon you;
and only from having been known as a kind of picture
beforehand will the plane deepen into the day and its
distances. And so with coming indoors (after descending
from the mountaintop, say, or breaking out of the woods,
crossing the hot, August meadow and entering the
darkened room) — only then can you find respite from the
coarseness of actual mileage, or of space thickened into
crudity by substance. Only then will the canny flatness of
dark engravings, the contingent depth of heavy painted
brushstroke, the world of surfaces turned inward — only

then will these comfort and refresh, and unfetter the mind that had for so many hours remained imprisoned in the body's meditation through space.

This is true of all interiors and exteriors. What is so peculiar, then, about my vision of the world from *here,* from these chambers (whose doors swing windily on their hinges like turning leaves of vellum)? Actually, we might consider these places — to which, as I said, I seem more and more to be returning — as, for example, pages in a notebook. Mostly opaque, yellowing at the edges, dumb, insensible — just as space itself is — unable to reflect, from their rough outer surfaces, anything more problematic than the shadow of my pen projecting from a sort of cat's head-like form of shadowed fingers curled about it. Paler than the maples' barren leaves outside. I could never see the darkened lawn, the distant sea, the even farther distant mountains, by means of such pages — by any usual, papery means. I could not look through them (as through the excitingly noisy, wrinkled, colored "cellophane" of my childhood, at a world suddenly reddened with angry knowledge, or yellowed into the fragile scene of skeptical regard). I could read nothing in the self-absorbed faces of such pages — no figurative mirrorings, no depictions, only the shadowing of moving fingers. How could I know the world "in" or "by" such notebook pages as those to which I have likened the old place I have come back to?

*

To see the world through the spectacles of text, then . . . Not to be blinded by frozen language to the light of what it designates, no. Nor to learn *of,* or *about,* as if that were to encounter. When I wrote long ago of The Poet:

> One impulse from a vernal Book
> Taught him much more of Man
> Than any nature walk he took
> Or any risk he ran

— I mocked those who don't know that Experience itself is indeed a word, and that (beyond even that) I meant it literally. But the joke has been on me, for this is not a matter of teaching. But look — here is the page: there is the world. The first maps the second, opens it up like a book or a door, illuminates its daylit darkness, makes coherent its insane flux, and so forth and so forth. But all these are evasive figures. What happens is that you read the page, you cry out against its particular folly and madness, your outcry is mirrored in the echoing sounds of what is Out There — the sounds by which it asserts its vast indifference to, and difference from, what is said of and in it — and you are reassured of your sanity.

So that is how — to return from this analogy of the notebook page to the reality of where I am now — this house, this weekend cottage which is becoming more and more a place of business, becomes the locus of all placing. The agency of central intelligence. The head of the matter and the heart of the page.

*

— Later that same afternoon: the trace of black I noticed in the entry before this last one seems a bit longer now, vertically, than I had remembered it. Is it casting its own lengthening shadow? I must measure it for future reference. Let's see — there! about .5 millimeters. We'll see.

*

I have come back here, after several days, at midnight. Or rather — my watch having stopped — at what should be close to midnight, give or take a few hours. Without the ticking of a clock, like the blind tapping of a cane in the darkest spaces of the day, I can only guess how far along we have come in the course of night. I cannot see the faintly — the inaudibly faintly — humming clock of the stars, even on a clear, moonless night. And the light shed by the streetlamp outside my window, unlike the sunlight, does not modulate its quality or its way of painting shadows, over the range of its hours. From where I am now, night's interior is indivisible and the point, the exact point of just midnight, is buried in a stack of darkness.

Thoreau remarks of these dark, indeterminate hours that "I know not whether I am sitting on the ruins of a wall, or the material which is to compose a new one." I too speak out of the night, out of this place whose walls crack slightly, like old buildings. The lost point of midnight would be the point of turning the old into the new — the slow trip down the left arm of the parabola there becomes the journey up the right one. In my own place of night, locked away from the considerate, time-telling starlight, it may be that I am moving deeper into silence, or perhaps out into the noise of daylight: only were I aware of the moment of reaching midnight's turning-point could I know which.

Yet even more. It may be that upon that one point pivots the whole vast paradigm itself, the axis of all axes. At the darkest point it should then be decided not only whether one was entering or emerging, but where the meaning was to lie, how the values were to be assigned. After all, every turnabout is yet one more step downward, through the long day of nights and days, toward the darkening of their very alternation, the twilight of movement between the deep tunnel and the opening plain.

And yet we have awakening to fresh light; the dimming of the guardian streetlamp which nurses our ignorance of when at night it is; the rising of the humming wind — each of these is the only rebirth I would trust in anyone. The more of this kind, the merrier; the more successive reborn mornings we pass through, the truer each has been. I scorn the self-deceived, meretricious sort of turnabout, the midnight at broad noon, the flash of conversion: there can only be one of these flimsy moments in each life, lest repetition wreck its fragile uniqueness and unmask its glitter. So Saul stumbled on the way to Damascus, had a fit outside Antioch, swooned at Laodicea, passed out at Tyre, and on and on — each vision confirmed more completely than the last the insignificance of the first one. To be born from above — *gennêthênai anôthen* — this is a mistranslation of life itself. The high rebirth — being born again each day from the windy dawn and the water of the early dew — this is what we have. Each successive morning confirms our first one. We ignore the truth of this at our peril.

Now: a braying klaxon, a screeching siren. These tear at the silence, like a deadly tocsin, calling us to thoughts of

outrage and of pain. They are somewhere out there, out-
side of where I am now. I had better lock this house up for
the night again.

*

Just before I put out the light last time, I notice the vertical
mark on the first blank — or rather blankened — page. It
seemed darker than it had been before, and slightly wider
at the top. Today I turned to it again: the widening is
clear; the mark hangs like a tiny nail, or teardrop. My
reading glass and ruler tell me that it has indeed grown in
length, as well as intensity — it must extend close to one
millimeter by now. Is this some kind of dark gray mildew?
some other fungus? Is this mark a disease, literally, of the
paper? Perhaps it will continue to grow.

I remember being here last week and writing something
about walls — about interiors and exteriors, perhaps. But
the great advantage of the way I live here now is that I am
free of my own influence. Not being able to read what I
have previously set down disobliges me from attending to
it. We are usually in necessary bondage to what we have
just that moment written: certainly our English syntax, our
headlong flight from subject through predicate, leaves its
terrible traces of commitment. I — and note that I must
follow myself, my "I," with a verb, lest I remain alone im-
prisoned in the sound of half a lamenting scream: *Ai*
severed even from its self-echoing "ai" or "aye." No: "I"
must be interpreted by its succeeding verb, if only by *must*.
And so every word we write must look back warily — if not
in outright fear — at the syntactic demands made on it by
What Has Gone Before. It is altogether fitting and proper
to our condition that this emblem of our bondage (to our
former selves, our own childhoods, our decisions of last
year's noon that have cast us into tonight's dungeons) reap-
pear. It breaks out like a clanking chain, hung in a dark
catenary of inverted rainbow, whenever we make sense on
paper.

My ink disappears completely only about two words
behind me; in no case can my words escape the chain gang
of our grammar. Yet I am beautifully free of a larger com-

mitment to read what I have already written here. That I have been at work in this place there can be no doubt at all: I am now on (in?) page 51 — as the blue, stamped digits on its upper right-hand corner maintain — of this old ledger (bought at the Harvard Coop, November 1946), filled with various youthful embarrassments up to page 28. The next right-hand page is blank, save for that tiny, vexingly growing mark (it looks like this now: ᴛ), and so are all the others, all but "all but" of 51 included (and now even that clause isn't strictly true any more).

So: I have indeed been writing. But coming back to this place at various times of day or night now is a unique kind of visiting. I have strong memories of this house, but it is a place with nothing in it but the desk, the lamp, the notebook, the chair — a house empty, that is, of all save itself. My memories of having been here, then, are my own misrepresentations only: they are not shared by the sentimental objects which usually evoke cluttering remembrances. Consider an ordinary sort of room. There is the bed. There are someone else's shoes (and there is no proximate arrangement of two shoes which can avoid emblematic pathos, empty shoes — and perhaps hats — being the only memorials of presence we have now that are unfilled by body the way corpses are emptied of soul). There, the view of Rome on the far wall (a remembered purchase, an outgrown taste, a fantasy on remembered themes exhaled by remembered spots); there, the abandoned novel with the pages still turned down. (What had happened that afternoon that made one stop at "The Marquise chose not to go out, after all"?) All these things have minds of their own, tugging away at our consciousness of them, and doing much of our remembering for us.

But none of that here. There are only these bare walls framing empty spaces, and the faint, transitory shadow cast by the ghost of what I have just been writing. To be locked up here for the rest of my life would be comforting, but intolerable — if only because so much liberty, so much independence of what I had said, what I had done, before a few seconds ago, could not be borne for too long. That's why I must close these pages now, switch off the lamp, leave the house and enter the street outside, swarming and buzzing as it is with so many contingencies. It is like coming down — rather than up — for air.

*

Montaigne called it his *arrière-boutique,* the back of the store, the place you have to keep for — and to — yourself. Here it is: here am I. Or does this place keep me? I wonder, too, about the specific mode of "keeping" — as in, say: *During those years he kept a journal some of whose pages are still in the possession of Fräulein Traum* — that kind of keeping. Perhaps all of the following kinds of keeping are somehow concentric:

"He kept the keys to the apartment on a chain around his neck. Fortunately, they were small."

"He kept an apartment in the West 60s — it had an oblique view of the park."

"He kept a mistress whose constant betrayals of him, in that very apartment, were somehow in keeping with the nature of his devotion."

"He kept a small notebook in a drawer of the table beside the bed, a notebook which, if he couldn't keep hidden from her, about which she kept silent."

"He kept, in that small notebook, a diary, which, in turn, kept him in bondage: to the keys, the whole place, her, the diary itself, the truth, and all of the lies with which the truth keeps being told."

*

I keep time in this place, and faith, and hold of something: I keep up, — up with, — on, not to speak of — down and — out. The point of all this is not to let go.

*

The mark on page 29 keeps growing larger, and darker. It now looks like this:

T

Was I thinking of Keeping the last time I was here? So I
seem to remember. Something I have surely kept as I have
been able to keep nothing else — not even my unmodulated
identity — is something I have kept *from*. For example: the
Novel, the undoubtedly very great novel I have never
read — have, indeed, kept at arm's length all these years.
The Novel is one whose greatness I totally acknowledge,
having read many of its author's other books, having
trusted for years the multitude of reports, commentaries,
reminiscences, and citations of it. I know the names and
some of the actions of the major characters. The power of
certain episodes, the meditative sweep, the almost
mythopoeic description of the major cities, the great con-
trast between the two different countrysides, the inter-
penetration of character and fate and its final turnabouts,
the concluding meditation on death as figured in the
reader's experience of feeling only one last leaf under his
page-turning forefinger — I know all these with the purity of
hearsay and the intensity of my own reconstruction. It is as
if the Novel had been lost long ago, and certain fragments
discovered by me in a long-unopened closet upstairs and
brought to light, but only to the light of my own desk
lamp. The Novel would then be in my keeping. A
bibliophile might possess the Novel in all its editions, print-
ings, translations, and so forth. But I keep — in my way of
keeping — all the individual copies ever printed, or ever to
be printed, anywhere, as well. The word "keep" has never
meant anything other than *seize, guard, hold*; and yet this
Great Book came into my keeping through no direct act of
appropriation. One *seizes* a book from a shelf or a table,
guards it while reading, *holds* it peculiarly in memory — there
is, at any rate, always the moment of taking. In this case,
however, the Novel came to me slowly and almost imper-
ceptibly: I had always "meant to read it," but after a certain
number of years, I began deliberately to "save it up" for
something — a sea voyage, a long illness, a spate of jury
duty during which, for various reasons, I would never

actually be impaneled. Then, keeping it saved up gradually became an end in itself. It was as if a forever-unread, indeed canonical, version of the Novel had somehow been left in my keeping. And there — here — it still is.

There are only two things left to be said of my keeping that book by keeping it from me, and me from it. First, there is the question of expense: what has my possession cost me? What will, in the end, the price have been? I cannot think of any reading I could give the Novel, any sequence of readings over the years, of rereadings, considerations, glosses — any experience leaving its track of marginalia — that could be more *attentive* or more responsible than my keeping of it. Second, there is, after all, my fear of loss: at any moment, a headstrong burglar, or a weak-spirited drug addict, could run off with what I have kept for so long. No matter who he was, he would be disguised as myself, and his breaking and entry would appear to an outside observer to be no more alarming than an act of pushing back a chair, walking across a room, sighing as I reached up to a shelf to take down a heavy volume.

All I have to keep myself from such an act of theft is my fear of dying at that very moment.

*

My bookkeeping is as peculiar as my housekeeping. These pages have no vertically ruled columns, and in my case, profit and loss, indeed all accounts, are settled at some higher level of auditing a moment after I set anything down here. What can I say of the book I keep? Is it a matter of personal accounts? the more abstract but powerful notion of real accounts? This journal is a book of first entry, but surely of last entry as well: a private and a general ledger. My bookkeeping is triple-entry. Whatever gets set down here is registered not only as debit and credit, but under my third category, the unruled column of interpretation. For the question is never of profit and loss, but, for each of my transactions between the attention and the world, the question of under which nominal account it will be entered. It is the question of what the entry itself, beyond even the transaction it records, will come to mean, even in the brief, legible time before it comes to light and thus invisibility.

*

Visible now, two days later, is this on page 29:

T

A letter T, perhaps, with its crosspiece flush against the up-per line? A strange position for it. This may be some sort of distressed watermark, turning itself out onto the page; but I doubt it. Why a letter T? Plutarch wrote learnedly and ingeniously on the meaning of the unexplained letter E inscribed at Delphi, offering various suggestions. But no learning and no wit can help me with the T that has gradually appeared where my own writing, in disappearing ink, first gave way to openness again. And I say *openness* because a silent, blank page is far from empty, but crowded with all the possibilities that could ever be imagined for it.

*

I have been thinking about the T: The beginning of a THE? The annunciation of a Noun to come? Its vertical bar has now reached the lower line, and I trust it will stop growing.

*

But of course, it did not. The bottom of the vertical has thickened into a serif, although unmatched by any others, or by points, figurative hands, or whatever, aiming downward from the ends of the crosspiece. But some T's are cut just this way:

T

I am only concerned now that *my* concern with this process should come to an end. Not because the whole matter is beginning to seem trivial and compulsive, but rather because the ambiguous mark, slowly descending into a significant clarity, is like a way of keeping pace with something, here in this room in which I have no clock, no

calendar. That aspect of it all is an intrusion. Now that the
T is almost complete, it is beginning not to matter so
much, and not to matter what it means. By the time it is
done with bringing itself into being, it shall not matter to
the mind at all. I await this with pleasure, but not with
undue eagerness.

*

A fugitive visit, late at night. But no longer, as formerly,
merely to *be* here, with all of what that has meant, and
could mean. I am only concerned for the completion of the
T, for the certainty of its emergence, for the end of my con-
cern. Neither do the pleasures in the tasks of dwelling in
this house, even from time to time, seem to count for
much. The T is there as it was yesterday: to observe just
this exhausts all my desire to be here now. I wonder what
is happening to me? Just before I glanced at that earlier
page, a bright light in the open window of a house across
the way beckoned to my attention. Even from where I sat
at the desk, barely turning my head, I could see into the
room — the curtains were pulled back to afford just such a
view into it — where there was a bed near the window and
three figures. Dressed in blue jeans and white shirts, the
two facing me, standing against the edge of the bed, were
young women: the third, seated on the bed, apparently
cross-legged, had its back to my view. The three presences
touched hands; then the two women started slowly to
caress, and then to unclothe the identically dressed person
on the bed, all the while intermittently opening buttons,
shedding sleeves, and climbing out of jeans and pants of
their own. Ordinarily, such a scene would have engaged
my erotic, dramatic, and sociological interests; but I found
that I cared not to observe even long enough to determine
the sex of the third, backward figure, let alone what
configurations of body would ensue, and what deeper ar-
rangements of intention, of power, of abstraction, change,
and pleasure might be read therefrom. I could only think of
my developing letter, my T (what shall I call it? my
character? my sign? my mark?). My absorption in it seems
to transcend and contain curiosities, desires, wonderings,

let alone appropriate ways of being in this place. I shall have done with it soon.

And it will have done with me. I must give over this excess of concern for the mark — given its slow rate of appearance, this rushing back up here at odd hours of the evening yields little information. Indeed, I am led to fancy undue extensions of the bottom serif, as if, under the pressure of too much attention, the form were beginning to change. But it is not. I must stay away from here for a while, and wait until a week of unchangingness confirms my ability to close the book, as it were, on this flyspeck (as I first thought it was) that has gotten out of control.

*

Have I caused all this, somehow, to be happening? The very appearance of the mark entered my relation to this place like an irrelevancy, and only gradually grew into (what? *importance*? that's not quite the word for it) — well, into What It Is Now. Like the modern kind of erotic impediment, those internalized versions of the impediments of Heroic Love (The Angry Duke Puts His Daughter in the Tower; Duty to One's People; The Pirates Capture Amaryllis and Put Her Ashore on Samos) form invisible barriers (imperfections in the Other lose their former homely loveliness; the Other's absence or presence loses distinctive outlines and becomes a blur; duty to a newly founded State: God Bless Oneself). And so forth. These arise, like the contrivances of a shallow plot, in the ordinary tale of the common. And this is what has happened to my life with this house, this room, this table, these pages — particularly the one open before me now, the absorbingly maculate face of page 29, whereon the T has been making its mark, the unvirginal blankness of the intervening leaves. Am I falling out of life (as "out of love") with all this? I have no love for the character, nor even any lust for it: its form displeases me, its potential significance so open as to be boring (what would living with T be like?), its role in the rest of my life unheroically ruinous. And yet my attention to it, even its very appearance, must in that case by my own fault. It would be childish to blame it on the page.

*

Without having looked at page 29, I have come back here, after two days, only to record that, without having looked at page 29, I have come back here after two days.

*

Any person of the world would infer that I have, during the past few weeks, been visiting other houses, facing other pages. I shall answer no questions, tell you no lies; I shall only say that the matter is not to be discussed *here.* Especially now. This is a matter of fidelity.

*

Well, there it is. A week has been more than long enough, and the whole matter has finally resolved itself, but in a way that I had not predicted. There is no reason to go about it: the T grew not a bottom serif, but literally, a bottom line, a lower crossbar exactly reflecting the upper one, in short

I

an emphatic, rhetorically extravagant, letter I. Not a pictogram for vision ("eye-beam") nor the meeting place of two bricks — nothing like that. It is the letter I with which I started to write these remarks in the sympathetic ink. The ink has redarkened into immortality; I has returned; I have turned on myself. All my good intentions for these pages have gone by the board, there being no question about the nature of the I. Its consequences, unlike the potential definite article, the implied noun, of T, are minimal. It is the I of It: it enters into the simplest and most direct grammatical shift, from first person to impersonal third, from subject to wholly othered object. And the final trace of the following letter, a lower-case t, has completed the whole life cycle of the mark. The *It* is that of the first two words with which I started what I had thought were these authentic, self-obliterating pages. "It works," I had written, of my disappearing ink. It does; but like some kinds of remembering and — worse — for some kinds of forgetting, not for long enough, finally giving us the lie. That will be it, by which we mean all.

In Place

The Way We Walk Now

It was not that there were only the old ways of going from one chamber to another: we had learned to imitate the noble walk of those who had built, and dwelt in, the Great Palaces, moving gravely through the interconnecting rooms; aware of the painted ceilings and the import of the images there for their lives, but never needing to look up at them; free among their footmen; roaming their spaces and yet by no means imprisoned in the fragile grandeur to which, in the afternoon light, the rooms had fallen. We had learned thereafter to mock that stiff way of walking, and after that, to replace it with our own little dances and gallops; we roller-skated from room to room, or occasionally bicycled. Being confined by the layout was not the point, nor was it what may or may not have happened to the houses — whether they were indeed in ruins or merely in need of repair. We had all gone away somewhere: off to war, or to the city, or had shipped out for the East. And those of us who returned, or who had stayed wherever it was, came quite naturally to go about in the field, or among the hills or through the streets. At first, it was almost with memorized maps of the ways rooms opened off each other, and of just what courts it was on which the various windows gave; after that, with no recollected plan, but always moving the better for having started out in one of the great houses.

But then it almost ceased to matter where we were. What had become necessary that we do by way of amble, or of hop skip and jump, had so taken over power from mere place that it generated the shapes of space through which it moved, like a lost, late arrival at the start of a quest who had set out nonetheless, dreaming each new region into which he wandered. Pictures of the old places still had a certain pathos; but they were not of ourselves or of our lives. The distance that had been put between us and the houses crammed full of chambers was utter, like that between the starry heavens above and the text below us, on the opened page.

A Week in the Country

A plague raged in the city. In a region nearby, August
fields were shivering under a very heavy rain, but for hours
before, the grasshoppers' buzzings had crowded into any
ear that could not escape listening, and the high, soft
thunder had been as easy to ignore as the rumors relayed
by Rube and Boob, the turnip farmers over the hill, and as
boring. In the house, a trapped wasp sang madly in the
windowpane, and softly butted the narrow glass with a
sound that was always on the edge of echoing a familiar
noise. But there is no story to tell: Village life had broken
down and the solitary heroisms of the simple women in
their flowering yards had faded into darkening pages. The
farms yielded their cash crops. Those who huddled in the
house during the long rain, and rekindled the stubs of blue
candle until there was power again, were not going to tell
old stories to pass the time as they sorted odd seeds in what
light there was, or silently sat out the important thunder. It
was as if they could not be prelude to any narrative that
would not be twisted out of shape as it awkwardly side-
stepped the embarrassments of its own unfolding, or strove
to avert its hearing from the creaking of hinges as its own
doors opened and shut. It was as if sheer place, unable to
act, reigned nonetheless, at a noble distance from what,
were it nearer, would be a foreground, and as if its genius
lay in this.

It was a wet September afternoon. Clear water dropped
from the barberry bush, as if distilled from the gouts of
redness themselves wept by the small green leaves. In the
brown soggy cornfield rose the coarse remarks of the crows.
Indoors, the lamp dropped warm light on the polished
brass of its own base, the fire hummed in the hearth, the
loudspeakers in the corners were aflame with Brahms. The
windows looked out, through the bushes, toward the gray
pond. The question that arose like a kind of mist concerned
the outdoors and the room: was something remarkable to
happen out *there,* whether glimpsed from within or
unheeded by whatever minds were moving about in the
half-darkness here in the flickering of the firelight? Or was
it going to be taking place inside the windows which, even
when open, remain blind to what is behind them? And
would the broad gray ground remain in its wet stupor, un-
mindful of what would be going on, and undeceived?
These were the matters that had crept up the page to the
top of the agenda; so that what it was that might hap-
pen — or even the heartbreaking truth of what it was going
to be happening in place of — first appeared to recede
behind the question of where. But by early evening that
question darkened and grew and absorbed all the other
ones to which, like night with her flock of shadows, it
finally seemed to have given rise.

About the House

In the high attic, all the old things had been accumulating meaning. Down in the basement were the pump, the furnace, the oldest masonry, the dark bottles of Pomerol settling slowly toward their prime. The difficulty of living in the house, in all the rooms between these, lay partially in trying to understand how moving up and down stairs between the floors was only a matter of changing levels, not of achieving any real elevation. There were forays made up to all the dusty hangings, the closed chests whose labels themselves, covered with dust, seemed to require labeling, the old pictures that looked somewhat grotesque as opposed to the remembered versions of them with which we were conversant downstairs. When there were descents down the cellar steps, it was because something was wrong, or something was being retrieved; we moved up into the spaces under the eaves, however, when there was nothing else to do. On the floors between, the significance of everything was one with its use.

Stepping out-of-doors — on an October afternoon, perhaps, whose brightness and touches of chill kept the edges of everything very clear — and looking back at the house from outside was something else again: anything it could lead us to conclude would be like a tale told by an abandoned house to some passer-by, who, if he retained any of the whole matter, would remember the interiors, the rooms, the passageways, which he had visualized from the story. He should have forgotten what the house looked like about which he had stopped on his walk to inquire. This is also somehow involved with the problems of living there.

Keepsakes

Only after eighteen years had passed was it possible to regard the bed and the three bullets in any relation at all to each other and to what had been decaying around them. A man had died in the bed, which was broad and strong and costly, and his widow gave it to the energetic friends. The bullets were small, heavy, .32 caliber cartridges, the clip that had held them long since lost, the enabling pistol long since sold by the widow, who had forgotten the last three cartridges. The energetic friends removed them for safekeeping, meaning to deal with them later on, with the effect that for years and years they rattled inside desk drawers, among staples and scissors, or in little boxes of paper or tin or leather. Their brass cases and copper noses grew dull. As they lost luster, they seemed to lose their meaning as objects, as if no concept could adhere to them, as if something inherent had leaked out of them and then perhaps dried from off their surfaces.

So that the problems posed by what they actually were — whether age had incapacitated them, and so forth — and by what they had been, and might be, for, ceased to seem pressing or even interesting. The only appropriate way of dealing with them consisted eventually in visiting them in whatever container they happened to occupy; handling them; perhaps even from time to time momentarily misplacing one or two, so that a short, nervous search had to ensue before one of them, duller than could have been expected, turned up at the end of a dark drawer. That they were those particular bullets, that there were three of them, that they were not exactly a legacy but had to be coped with nonetheless after their owner's death — these insistent and unimpressive facts inhered in their weight and in their familiar appearance, in the way they would lie rhyming like one-word lines, two of them parallel, the third slightly askew but with its tip touching the others. All this naturally obscured how during all that time they may have been acquiring an enormous importance of their own.

The bed and the widow entered a world of narrative, however. Just where this world touched that of the bullets — and, by inference, where these regions lay and still lie in relation to one another — is not easily perceived. One can imagine thinking, as he put on his spanking new solar topee, of the curves and returns of a dark river working through rain forest. One can think of previous encampments, of the traces of earlier explorations. And then there would be the narrative world itself. The first glimpse of it might come at sunset along the river, with lights beginning to appear at what might be a border station. And then one would begin to know what had gone on — not, surely, the events themselves (the widow remarried, then left her husband for new sadnesses, the bed consumed the lives of the energetic friends who lay in it until they fell apart) but the processes whereby one's things can objectify, can shrink as the moisture of ceremony leaves them for the general air.

In other words, the bed had always lain midway between the bullets and the widow, as if it were a text, neither person nor object. The widow might evaporate into hearsay. The bed was clearly becoming more and more like the bullets. And the bullets, dulled now to a final low tone past which they would not move, lay in whatever box it was, creating more and more of their own purity.

End of a Chapter

. . . But when true Beauty does finally come crashing at us through the stretched paper of the picturesque, we can wonder how we had for so long been able to remain distracted from its absence.

Dutch Interior

The light comes in from the window on the left, pearly and clear, but not if one is in the room that is in the picture. No indeed—from within, the light might seem more general, no matter where in the room the windows were, even as the contents of the room would cease to matter very much. The spotty globe, for example, upon which one could perhaps descry patches of the known world; the tapestry on the wall with its faded heroic figures; the lute laid face-down on the table, its belly and rosette averted from view; the girl in the fur-trimmed taffeta, plumply Dutch withal, who may or may not be there to be fiddled with, for a price; the dead nature of the leaden crystal carafe which both shines and does not; the whispers gleaming in some of the folds of the girl's skirt; even the mirror that does not show in the picture, or that may not be there at all, whether planar or hemispherical, the mirror that, one might have thought, would be another order of matter entirely—for one within the room, these are all mutable properties. They would, you see, be important only to a picture of the room, a piece of the outsider's wall which windowed on to—not into—the flat table of significances, its tropes of space.

But this being-in-the-room transforms everything. What matters from within is what there is room for, whose insignificance the viewer of the picture ceases to mind. There is a fable about this: *First there was room on the flat fields, in the bright northern air. Then they added an indefinite article to "room," something boxlike and embodying. Then they went into it with articles of furniture and virtue, which added the definite article, the "the" of this rather than of that.* The fable was originally found either on the back of a picture of the room, or else within, pasted to the back of a drawer in the dark sideboard. The fable itself gives no indication of its provenance.

The Old Pier-glass

It was as if, he thought, someone had censored the whole
of a well-meaning but naïvely loquacious wartime letter,
leaving about its cut-out center only a frame to be sent on
nevertheless, with needless earnestness, to its addressee.
Alas, it was even more as if the letter had announced a
death to begin with, and only the black borders and a little
white, by way of a mat within them, were left. For there
was in fact no glass in the old, heavily lacquered frame.
The carved wood surrounded only the dusty corner of the
corridor it stood in.

This in itself neither amused nor frightened him. But
what if he had had to consider a pair of mad brothers, clad
in identical nightgowns, fake moustaches and tasseled caps,
looking out at each other from either side of the empty
mirror-frame? He would have had to contemplate a trope
of imaging, of presence making creakingly do for the pic-
tures that are usually dragged in to replace whatever is
absent. It would be a matter of a person replacing a lost
replacement. Very, very funny at first, it would have to
come to him, this time, very fearfully indeed.

On a Book, Found Inland Far
for René Char

    The sea-beach, its imploring heartbeat: but all the found shells were dry with silence, the unsounding sky in pain of blue, and the sand a powdered mirror that still had the power to render the lost immensities of our speech, under a wind too fierce not to smash anything as large as leaves.

    What fresh water there was was imprisoned in our flesh.

[Portugal's Journal] December 16: We cannot remain absorbed merely in the plot, the action, for in the end it will all have probably meant nothing. Nor can we concern ourselves with an honorable record of the indeterminacies, the injections of boulder and underbrush that make surveying the clear field so difficult.

Neither the salty tale, then, nor the singing honey of meditation, of summing up among the interstices of events, will do. And yet there is no middle way, for we hum or whistle only to flee speech, we crave melody when the punch-lines have soured.

And even searching out a new state is too much a *geste,* a high-flown caper, too tied to planning, furtive purchases of equipment, recruiting at strange bazaars, exhausting dry runs. Action is so epigrammatic, discharging its meaning like a joke.

Every deed is a loss of consciousness; every act is a black-out.

The Board: Not Oui-Ja but Non-Nein

She gave a little shriek that almost rhymed with the sound that had startled her, the long squeak of the heavy bronze ashtray as it skated across the shining surface of Carrara marble. The ashtray smelt of metal and of cold cinders. Neither of the sounds scratched any lasting track in the afternoon air of the room. The narrowness was keen, but unengraved, and the pitch of her cry, the sliding of the ashtray, pointed even momentarily toward nothing in particular.

But after all, where might they have alighted? "On" the reflection of one or another of the guests as it was caught faintly by the marble? "In" a falling interval, decrescendo? No, and in any case we should be left to wonder, at best, in parallel: as, at thirty-thousand feet over Newfoundland's unclouded wild, an imponderable ruled line cuts across miles of what is gray and green below, the lady's hand in the subway is graced with a delicate line across its back. The lines are both too straight to be anything but scars. The enigma of one, the beauty of the other have long since devoured the pain of their creation. They had come to rest along themselves.

The Sense of Place

That is what it had been about all along, he
thought — not as he drove along West Floral for a mile or
so before turning off, but as he sat, later, still quite alone,
pushing the thick water tumbler, the empty ash-receiver,
the crumpled napkin, the unused fork, around the smooth
surface of the restaurant table. They composed themselves,
even without the legends and roadways of the blue map on
the paper mat, into a nameless region in which the way
things were out of scale hardly mattered. It was as if, with
an enormous dumb wisdom, the parts of the place were
aware of his composing hand and maintaining gaze. And
yet it was no awareness of his on his part which made the
place seem so compelling, which made him feel as if it were
beginning to reach out to him, showing him what there was
not, otherwise, to be seen. The smudged tumbler contained
what had once been the element of water, for example; and
the crumbs in their uncharted constellations were ripe for
new mythologies, tales of the metamorphoses of ruin,
dissolution and dropping. It was with a surprising delight
that he began to realize all this. He would eagerly await
the next place that came to him.

After Flood Damage

(Start with the sound of the brook) The sound of the brook
was as insistent as a hissing of nearby fire, and it cut such
a broad swath of audibility through the trees, that it
swallowed up, and made part of its own utterance,
whatever those agitated branches had to whisper. Which
was much, but which was not about much. *(Go on about the
trees)* The tale each pale-tongued leaf had to tell in response
to the wind's mindless and bullying catechism was no more
than a catalogue of complaints about that questioning.
(Mindless? bullying?) The wind was not of this place, had not
dwelt here long enough to play on the instrument of the
given. *(What about the water in the brook, then?)* A different
matter: the nymphs of rock had always been here, and
their films and veils and draperies were the sole and proper
emanations of their visibility. Or say that they possessed
the passing waters, while our poor leaves, multitudinous
and weak, were claimed by the nightriding rushes of wind.
*(Well then, what did the sounds of the water mean? what did the
brook say?)* None of us knew at the time, but that did not
untune the quality of our attention. *(So that one is to end with
the sound of the brook?)* One is to end with the sound of the
brook.

Crocus Solus

A sigh? No more: a yellow or white rupture of the cold
silent winter ground, the exclamation of such effort. Yet
unaccompanied by the echoing multitudes that hope
surveys; one only, and whether an accident or an example,
too important in its uniqueness to be considered important
for its meaning. O, spring will come, and one time it will
not, but what we are to know we will know from all the
various emblems crying, out of the grass, *vivace assai,* and
waving in the soft wind, *ô Mort.* One swallow of water
makes no summer of earth. One drop of darkness is no
sign of wine. One flower points to nothing but itself, a
signboard bravely hung outside the signpainter's. The
crocus of all points, lying along the river, that speak for
themselves is but one point of saffron or of snow. A sign?
O, more . . .

Something Wrong down at the Pond

One summer evening when the sky behind him was still
red with the remains of daylight, and the small green heron
was making sponking noises from across the pond, he came
down to the motionless water. He stood at the edge and
peered over the reeds through which the wind groped
hesitantly, not so much toward music as away from
stillness. He saw emerging from a shadow in the water,
framed by the infirm brightness of what, by inference, was
reflecting the heavens, a head. He moved: it moved; he
tilted his head toward his right shoulder: the image did, in
its reversed way, likewise. And so: and so; and more: and
more — until the rhythm of action and recognition gradually
began to slough off its false resemblance to cause and
effect, and just before the water darkened into a condition
below reflectiveness, the handsome youth realized with an
ambiguous thrill that it was indeed the head in the pool
which was reflected by the figure that was his own. It was
not tragic to discover that he was the image of something
more substantial than himself, something even less
accessible to his elicited reach toward it than a fragile
fiction floating in water might be to a desiring hand. It was
rather comforting to be absolved of the responsibility of
taking on either Knowledge or anything serious in the way
of Fate. Night closed in on the pond, making the matter of
the images deeply moot.

In Place of Body

The garden is a very singular one. It is not that it is difficult of access — although one is constantly told that there is only one way in, there are in fact many — but that this contingent availability is of its essence. A public garden, a private park — each of these not despite the other, but because of it. This place is always said to contain representations of the absent forms: branches of the oldest trees intertwine in the touches of marriage survived; vines embrace their props, not with the deadly cuddling of some ground-cover that has run to stifling excesses, but with the old grace of taking and giving support; stalks of flower push out through the earth, filling the holes they make and mixing root and matrix into an element of ground; the evening air caresses the soft curves of the turf. But as if this were not enough, the lap of the ground cradles a body of delight, the representation fitted to its primary form, the hills of the body embedded in the valleys of the shade. It is as if every word here were embracing the object it named. And then meaning would flourish, whether in absence or presence being of no matter now.

Figures of Speech. Figures of Thought.
Figures of Earth and Water.

Once upon a time, the old, wild synecdoche of landslides was frighteningly transumed when a mountain — Mt. Black — rolled downward like one of its own boulders, over the whole peaceless land. In metonymy meanwhile, beyond the other mountains, a mad sea was flowing somewhere, like a river.

The Boat

It took him away on some nights, its low engine running silently on even until he was too far out to hear it himself. It was as dark as the elements of water and night through which it moved. It was built for one: he was helmsman and supercargo both. It rode so low that he could roll into it from wherever it was tied up, and lie prone, his head perhaps turned to port. It responded surely and delicately to the controls, all accessible from where he lay. It headed out, but never back: he could not remember having come ashore from it. It was out of service for some years, after which he came to realize that his final ride on it, some night, would not be unaccompanied, that the boatman on that voyage would stay aboard, and that he himself would disembark at last.

Limping on Lemnos, on a Hill with Waves

    Picking himself up from the island ground, he began to move away from where he first found himself to be. All around him the dry rock plunged thirstily into the colorful water. But to no avail: the rock, the parched earth, the occasional olive tree all seemed to have been rejected by whatever there was in the sky that mitigated the hopelessness of its broad blue. What little there was here — the necessary conditions of land but without some of the final sufficiencies — was enough to receive an original visitor, a lame god falling out of the heavens. And a later traveler, put ashore on this acutely avoidable place, might move with an irrelevantly parallel halting. And following these, anyone moving across this unshadowed slope, swatted by the lashing heat, would be claimed by some defective rhythm. So that what he began, with a misleading slowness, in fact to flee was not to be found in a cave, or among some whitened ruins along the sea. It was the whole place that was a kind of frightening effigy.

The wind had blown his hair about and then gone on to inquire among the remaining leaves on the trees behind him. Otherwise, the rise of ground on which he stood was bare — rock, whitish grass, cold earth: these and the gray of the sky were as frames for each other, the conditions of picturing without a picture, presentations of presentations but with no meaning to be transferred. But what he saw as he looked toward the horizon was another matter. The scene pictured itself; the hills, the sky poured down among them, the breaks in the clouds all glossed the statement of sheer distance. The wind returned and whistled a refrain among the grasses: it was the only tune that it could play. He had taken up a place in which he could come to terms with the lie of the land.

The Dancing Shadows

A walker along the half-lit avenues that night would most probably have noticed nothing unusual as he moved amongst the returning throngs, thinned out somewhat by the raw weather and the emergence of the late hour from the bustle of the day's end. Dropping snow softened the yellow light that fell across the sidewalk, meaninglessly, from grim and glaring lamps. One walker perceived the multiplicity of his shadows in this kind of light: they lengthened, shortened, blended, superimposed themselves upon each other's paling ghosts, and generally made light of the power of one's shadow over one's substance. How they danced with each other, these mere images, before they vanished in the caverns of flat snow opened up by other lights! Like all the other walkers, and the dexterous snowflakes, and the cars moving by down the avenue in the other direction, the shadows of shadow were all part of the poetry of here and there. Neither sacred to this place, nor totally accidental to it.

"August, 1946: Back from Nantucket on the upper deck of
the ferry. A hot night, scraps of light remaining in the sky, as
if of a few high lengths of cloud, long after sunset. I do not
concern myself with their location astern — which is rather
peculiar for residual light of that kind — nor with the utter
darkness of the west into which we are headed. There is
laughter from the deck below, a quiet continual throbbing of
buried engines and the hoarse breathing of our wash. I stand
at the starboard rail, sadly shunning others. Then the rags of
radiance above awaken, yawn, stretch, gradually gather
themselves into long pale bolts and begin to unroll slowly and
extravagantly. Some are greenish, some are the bluish white
of skimmed milk. Toward the horizon they thicken into
serpentine folds of heavy drapery, flicked by the passing
shoulder of something vast into waves that move forward yet
do not advance. Then the fingers of cold dull red begin to
grope for the zenith, pointing into it and pushing it farther
away. The sky is wild with their light . . ."

— All of this went on and on, finally growing pale seem-
ingly at the same rate at which all the motion slowed even-
tually, colors fading into a glowing dimness against the dark,
until, at a moment that could have come along almost
anywhere during the period of five minutes it marked the
middle of, a long slow streak of white meteor shot through the
pallor above, a gasp of luminosity, a revision of wonder and a
reduction of what had been seen to a sign. Ironic, clear,
distinct; vector of agency against a scene; short, pointed, a
stretch of high path heading downward . . . well, I was young
and foolish and unable to know — as with everything else I
had ever been given — the nature of the gist. The bright track
of the Perseid was short, but long enough to lead into the vast
space of darkness between sky and sea. It has taken me thirty
years to remember the mockery of its accidence, thirty years
to recompose the prior light.

Not Something for Nothing

What he had begun only lately to notice was this: that he had always noticed relatively little of what was going on inside of, and among, the things he encountered; and this led him to recall noticing always what he had already possessed himself of: shining objects of memory. So that when, for example, he passed by something growing, something that had or had not bloomed yet, he would have had to wander back into the bright mountain meadow all ringed about with high pines and where all the names grew, to pluck a flower of designation and bear it back, through the shadowy woods, to the spot of attention. And it was because he could notice so little that he was able to call attention to things so startlingly sometimes. His mind was always wandering. He could point the way home.

— So that we have, after all, to be grateful that our light lies broken in pieces: were we to have to live in the generality of it, without the beneficence of the shady (no matter how questionable now, always), it would be unbearable. Perhaps if everything were to be reconstituted along with it, perhaps if the flashes of acknowledgment so scattered among us were finally to be reconvened, we might manage it all. But as it is, the very breaking-up of the radiance that might have for ever remained a deep ground was what will always cause us to have embraced these discrete fragments — turning on and off, fading, ending in a border of darkness — as with the arms of our heart.

A View of the Ruins

A short walk up from the hotel brings one to a place
more than half way up, from which the whole site is visible
and the different areas more discernible than from their
midst. Toward the left, an ancient grove will appear to
throw shadows more substantial looking than the trees
themselves. The cool colonnade seems even from such a
height to echo with long-departed footsteps; across from it,
the stoa may be perceived, with its rather boring porch. An
ancient upended tub (to the right of the stoa) is still in-
habited by dogs. Nearby was the tasteful garden. The
whole place was once busy with meaning and the bustle of
life, and when one looks over the whole matter from above,
the various areas can seem to have been plausibly engaged
with the living day. It is only from among the excavations
that the point seems lost — indeed, as the local saying goes,
"The overview, lest nothing be overlooked!" As to what
these ruins have to do with our lives, our problems and
headaches, our terrors and representations, each traveler
will of course determine for himself.

A House in the Tropics

New York. Cold. Cold everywhere. Cold in all the warm places. Cold in the interstices between adjacent blocks of cold. Cold at the heart of cold, and at the heart of the word "cold", and at the cold heart of the word "everywhere". But no — somewhere there is a dream of warming, and out of the warm blue comes a slow interisland steamer, visiting palm-ringed bays, putting off one sort of goods and taking on another, going from port to port much as one might proceed, errantly, from adventure to adventure without being aware of the cycle of tasks they comprised. And once launched into that heat, one might move from dream of place to dream of place, from house to house, without suspecting that there was a final one that one had been inevitably approaching. The House of Shells, full of ornaments so gorgeous that one never tried, before moving on, to listen to them; the House of Fruit, where warmth and sweetness dwell in a mild way; the House of Distance which, to whatever island one came, was always there, even if only as a low, unprepossessing hut. (On some islands, this was locally thought of as the House of Place Itself, but this resulted from an ancient linguistic error.) It was not that, down there, things and places resembled each other more, but that the warm climate did something to their modes of signifying. Their ways of meaning what they did, these places, were comely.

Memories of the Grand Tour

I was young then, of course, and could not know what it all meant, even though delight and instruction ran joyfully together along the boulevards, down the dark passages and out onto the hot, bright, silent squares. Else I should have recorded the whole journey in all of its continuing life; it is not, you see, to be revived in any way, and can only schematically — and perhaps thereby somehow horribly — be reconstructed from the pictures. (I mean those accomplished water-color sketches that travelers would learn to make, less like snapshots than like guarded time exposures, souvenirs rather than recollections; but no matter.) What I am left with even now is only the sense of moving from place to place, savoring each one the while thinking of the portion of the journey that yet lay ahead. I think now — but did not remember at the time — of my childhood: at the movies on Saturday afternoons, the light from the screen is reflected on my face, halfway through the Western, feeling the pleasure of the moment and the more prudently taken delight in the feeling of the remainder of the film, the shorts, the gangster movie, all yet to come, all still unconsumed.

And so it was with this: the high point of beginning at the place of the clear pools, the color of the sky and of ancient wisdom. Then the shells of the sounding beach; after that, the trek inland to the speaking well of the oracle, below the long, fragrant hill. Then I came, as one usually did, to the promontory below which lay the long reach of the whole land — the beautiful hills, the curving plain below that reached down to the forested area and the hidden mound. It was never purely the pleasure of the moment, nor the anticipatory joy of what one would reach next and next after that. It was the gradually unfolding nature of the entirety that could make one take so seriously such a conventional old trip, even though that unfolding would only be perceived long afterward, when the entirety could be completed because finally and fully imagined, rescued from the cold gaol in which failing memory, in her filthy smock, caressed and clucked over the fractured pieces.

Asylum Avenue

Here is a region through which you move, yet which
moves through you as you make your *paseo*. It is as if it
were receptive to the space you bring along with you, and
as if all the spaces flowed into each other like clear, green
water. It is itself a wide walk past heavily meaningless cars
and their motion, descending in curving and gracious
declines into the business of being a street. Yet it never
needs to become a mere boulevard, broadly proclaiming
itself over buried and forgotten bulwarks, but remains the
extension of what it comes toward, which itself kindly
advances to meet what has been moving forward at it for so
very long. It is the neighborhood of points of refuge
through which you pass: they continually astonish you with
their inventiveness; with the manner in which food and
drink have been tucked away in them; with the devices by
which you may see and not be seen. And suppose that
there was an encounter to be had there (I think of a
recently dead friend appearing at your door, his arms full
of books and papers, in place of someone else you had
invited, cheerfully assuring you that the reports of his
sudden death in Italy were quite mistaken) — it would be as
much part of your walk as your very setting out. It would
not be occasional. Nor would the sidewalk along the
asphalt shore constitute a road. It would be a way of
getting to work.

Building a Tower

It is because of what one has not found — a tan silo
pushing up beside the gambrel roof of a stone barn; a
square, ruined tower, Frankish, stone, backed on a pine
grove and overlooking the hot sand toward the calm blue
water; a dark, shingled cupola inspecting the wild, gray
sea; an unused wooden water-tank atop a penthouse facing
westward beyond the park; an obsolete lighthouse near the
mouth of the bay — of what one has not been able to adapt,
that one has to build. One can plan and plan for years, but
in the end the finished structure will always remain
somewhat surprising: it will have to seem, always, to have
been come upon, in a middle distance, from a dark walk,
the wanderer enwrapped in his study of the failing light
and what arises within it. It will always have to keep its
own distant appearance: even as one looks out, after years
of keeping it, through one after another of the windows —
toward the fire of sunset, out across the noon fields, into
the cold rain dripping from bare boughs — there must be at
least one window, however narrow, out of which one can
see what one looks toward the tower for. One must be
amid all that — dark books shadowing the interior walls,
bright vineyards lying toward the river outside — amid what
has always been, and will be, beyond.

In Place of Place

First of all, the original enclosure within which was our everywhere: it became, when we had to leave it, nowhere that was or was not to be. All the places we would have we would also have to take not as recompense, but just as images which eternity can nurture. Even if we could gather them all together, they would not compose what was less merely image; their designatum — the lost spot for which all our locations stand — would go on being merely what it is. As, for example, pain — piercing, throbbing or flickering — is a trope for the knowledge of that spot which we could not leave unplucked.

Well, then, To recapitulate: the earliest places are all taken away — the bright morning beach and the reddening late sand; the small stark sickroom; the caves in the merry rocks of childhood; the upright piano that loomed high above; all the Kinderscenen *inscribed in Albums for the Old. Nothing is given back; it is only that everything follows, making a kind of replacement in time. The space of these places has gone away, leaving only room for representations. The places that follow, far ones and near, momentary and familiar, are themselves representations: of the lost places? Yes. Of people? Perhaps. Of ourselves? Usually.*

So that everywhere we visited, every area wherein we may have been said to dwell, turned out in time to be bases we had had to touch, acceptances of what the world, madly gesturing as we moved about it, may have meant by its unagreed-upon signals. Every valley was also a picture of somewhere else we had not yet been to; each monument we climbed to the top of went away and left room to be remembered, but the memory would always fill up another space, the site of its late blossoming.

And, finally, there is something right about the vagrancy of the replacements. Nowhere can keep us for too long. Let us look at it this way: for want of the fruit the garden was lost, for want of the garden the places were gained, for want of the places new places arrived, for want of new places we dreamed and we dreamed. We composed in the tiniest inner room all the chambers of the endless palace, opening on to each other, directly as well as indirectly, off unlit corridors, once entered and left, then lost, even if returned to at a later time and by a route that we could never have known to be circuitous. And each room a place of mistakenness, so much so that while we are in it, there is no way of getting it right. Once left, there is only what we say of it, which is never mistaken.

There must be some way of learning from this about the last replacement, which is not of picture for place nor of place for picture; which is not like filler, unpainted terra-cotta smoothed into the space between places — interrupting the line of the dancer's drapery but not feigning, with a curious false art, where it was to go; which is not, in fact, anything occupying any space at all. Nor is it a matter of everywhere becoming empty space, waiting patiently — and with whatever wisdom was supposed to have been a version of — to be occupied by the new everywhere again. It is the replacement of space itself, of that space within which place has its being, with what will never again leave room.

Notes

In Time

"An Inchstone": *Wocheszeit* is a weekly memorial celebration.

"Half-Empty Bed Blues III": The mythographer's mistake by which Time, or Chronos, was given the scythe of the harvester Kronos, or Saturn, has been chronicled by Erwin Panofsky.

"When Song Will Not Do": See Schubert-Müller, *Die Schöne Mullerin*, song 11, "Mein."

"An Introduction to Absence": Cf. Fulke Greville, *Caelica*, 45 and, at the end, Catullus 85.

"A Talk in the Park": *Paradise Lost*, IV. 639ff.

"Vintage Absence": As of publication, the 1961 Medoc is all gone.

"The Fetch": A fetch is a spectral presence sent on a ghostly errand. The mythological golem was destroyed after the first letter of the word *emeth* ("Truth"), marked on its forehead, was removed, leaving the word *meth* ("Dead").

"From a House Party": Audrey G. was a friend. James Robertson Justice was an actor.

In Place

"The Way We Walk Now": This is perhaps about prose, as well as about life after verse. It introduces what start out to be stories, but get lost, amid other things, in the telling.

"A Week in the Country": No ten days of story-telling here.

"Translation from the French": Theories of narrative are theories of nothing.

"The Board: Not Oui-Ja but Non-Nein": *Oui* (French) + *Ja* (German) formed the original trade-mark of this parlor game.

"Crocus Solus": A single flower for Harry Mathews, Walter Abish and Raymond Roussel.

"The Boat": The bed (with memories of *A Child's Garden of Verses*).

"Limping on Lemnos, on a Hill with Waves": Hephaistos, flung from Olympus, hurt his foot when he landed on Lemnos.

"A View of the Ruins": Some readers may take this as the site of the philosophies (academics in the grove, peripatetics, dogged cynics, boring stoics, etc.).

"Memories of the Grand Tour": Whores used to — and perhaps still do — offer, for a special fee, "a trip around the world."

"Asylum Avenue": A poet walked to his office along this street in Hartford.

John Hollander, awarded the Bollingen Prize for poetry in 1983, is A. Bartlett Giamatti Professor of English literature at Yale University. He has published fifteen books of poetry, including *Spectral Emanations* and *Powers of Thirteen,* and several books of criticism, including *The Figure of Echo* and *Vision and Resonance.* His *"Blue Wine" and Other Poems* is also available from Johns Hopkins.